Fundamental Analysis
of Banking Sector

-:: Authers :: -
Vishvnath Y. Borse
Tajuddin S. Shaikh

PUBLICATION

Green Flag Foundation, Sonasan,
Sabarkantha, Gujrat-383210

ISBN 978-93-84570-74-3

i

Copyright: Author

© **Vishvnath Y. Borse And Tajuddin S. Shaikh**

First Publication: October - 2015

ISBN 978-93-84570-74-3

Typing & Design
Bharat B. Patel
Excellence Computer, Himatnagar

: Printing & Binding :
Manohar Book Binding, Himatnagar

: PUBLISHED BY :
Green Flag Foundation, Sonasan,
Sabarkantha, Gujrat-383210

Price: Rs.165/-

Preface

Currently, Indian economy was just crossed the 18000 benchmark and it is going to become the third largest economy in the world by 2008 after US and China as per the leading economist Dr. William T. Wilson.

Banking sector is also contributed to economic development, so it is very important sector for all country. We know that if anybody wants to sustain in this current economy than they want good return on their investment with consideration of inflation rate of an economy. Investment in the equity market is very risky compare to the debt instruments mutual funds. So, it needs in depth analysis of the scripts. The study of the stock market has become divided in to two kinds of thoughts: Fundamental Analysis and Technical Analysis.

Fundamental Analysis focuses on the economic forces of supply and demand that cause prices to move higher, lower or stay the same. Technical Analysis is the study of market action, primarily through the use of charts, for the purpose of forecasting future price trends. The term 'Market Action' includes the two principal sources of information available to the technician- price and volume.

Our Study base on banking sector and very good opportunity in future for the investor for invests banks scrip in India. This project report contains the information regarding fundamental of the scrip of Indian banking Industry. We collected data from the various web sites, annual report of the company, magazine books and news papers. We have completed economic analyses, Industry analysis & Banks.

Table of Content

1. Objective

➢ To study the financial scenario of the major banking company in India i.e. State bank of India, ICICI bank, HDFC bank and Bank of Baroda.

➢ To understand the effect of performance on price of its share and clearing awareness among investor.

➢ With all this such project is very much important to find out suitable investment opportunity in banking sector in India.

➢ To provide guideline to the investor for invest in banking sector in India..

➢ To able to provide and express the theoretical as well as the practical gained knowledge in the best possible manner.

➢ To prepare the report in a simple & descriptive manner so that any person can understand the analysis & report very easily and clearly.

2. Methodology

The methodology of the creation of the report shall follow the following steps, sequentially;

➤ Get a basic practical idea about the stock market & the leading sectors of it & its dealings.

➤ To study and analyse the external environmental factors (Macro) like Economy in order to get an idea as to whether the future is good for the investment in stocks or not?

➤ To study the scrip's of banking sector Companies like SBI, ICICI, HDFC, BOB & their balance sheet, P&L, etc. in an in-depth manner by means of ratio analysis to find out the sustainability and profitability of the company on basis of the past records

➤ Providing the final conclusion as to the portfolio which will be best for the current as well as future time span investment, keeping in mind the present reflecting factors that are affecting it.

3. Introduction

What is a Stock Market

Stock exchange is a place where the second-hand stocks are sold and bought by the people directly or via brokers through places called terminals. The fresh issued stocks are only available from company either through an IPO (initial public offer) or another issue. Later these shares can be sold in the same market.

To start trading in shares, one has to open a Demat A/c in a bank that works as a gate-pass for you in trading. It's always advised to first test your hand on the recent market trend by some simulation or in virtual world, instead of putting money into the market. When you are sure enough about technique and instincts, then you can shift to top gear with the bulls-n-bears.

The DO's & Don'ts in Stock Markets...

1. Always trade with a reasonable amount so that you can always have a smooth liquidity with you and with a piece of mind. In other words, bite only as much as you can chew!

2. Never follow rumors and if you listen to someone else, he may get you IN right time, but be sure whether he will be there to tell you when to get OUT?

3. Make sure that after investing; you regularly assess your shares portfolios to keep up with the recent changes and trends.

4. Don't make your analysis for short term only, but always have a consistent plan to follow.

The theory is that most successful traders are those that use market sentiments i.e. if too many people are bullish about the market to go up, the market is ripe for a decline, as they take profits or are forced to get out. Conversely, if too many people are bearish about the market, it implies that an up move may be in the making.

Rules for Dealing in Stock Market...

Each deal is the resultant of the demand of one hand satisfied by the supply of the others hand and for that, knowing the basic rules of volume analysis becomes very important which are stated below:

1. When the prices are rising and the volume is increasing, the present trend will continue and the price will be rising.
2. When prices are rising and volume is decreasing, the present trend is not likely to continue i.e. the price rise will decelerate and then turn downwards.
3. When prices are falling and volume is increasing, the prices will continue to fall.
4. When prices are falling and the volume is decreasing, the present trend is not likely to continue, i.e. the price decline will decelerate and then price will turn upward.
5. When volume is not rising or falling, then the effect on price is neutral

What is Index

The stock index is an odd four figure number that acts as a barometer of the state of the economy. The two basic stock indexes of India are SENSEX (the index of BSE) and NIFTY (The index of NSE).

A stock market index reflects the overall behavior / returns / movements of the equity markets as a whole. Some of its main objectives are:

1. The returns on the market index ideally represent the returns obtained on any standard portfolios.
2. The second use of an index could be in the form of a benchmark for measuring fund performance. An index with a good track record makes an ideal benchmark for fund managers to compare the performance of their funds and portfolio.
3. The third use of an index is that it can be used to trade derivatives and for launching index based products and funds

Nifty

Period	Value
10 October 2007	5428
10 March 2008	4777.80
10 June 2008	4162.20
10 September 2008	4482.30
14 October 2008	3303.20

Value

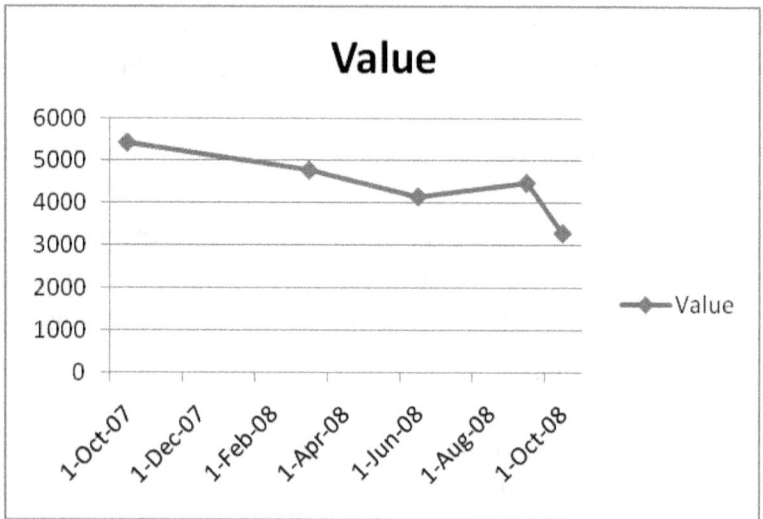

Sensex

Date	Closing
Jan 1 2008	20300.71
Jan 21 2008	17605.35
Mar 17 2008	14809.49
Mar 3 2008	16677.88
Jan 22 2008	16729
Feb 11 2008	16630.91
Jun 20 2008	14571.29
Jun 27 2008	13802.22
Aug 27 2008	14944.97
Oct 10 2008	10720.65
Oct 13 2008	11110
Oct 16 2008	10809.12
Oct 18 2008	9975

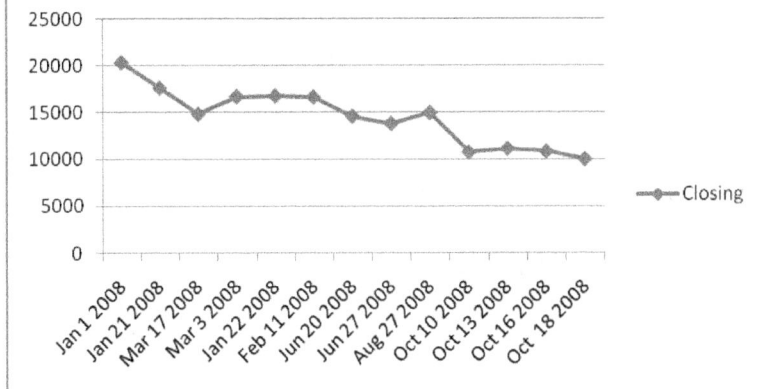

BSE Bankex

Bankex was launched by BSE to track the performance of the leading banking sectors as bank stocks are emerging as a major segment of the stock market. The base date for BANKEX is 1st January 2002 and base value for BANKEX is 1000 points. Bankex Index includes 12 selected major stocks which represent total 90% market capitalization of all the banking sector stocks listed on the BSE.

Period	Value
10 oct 2008	5,319.50
11 sep 2008	7210.66
22 Aug 2008	7009.69
14 jan 2008	12678.98
11 oct 2007	9570.79

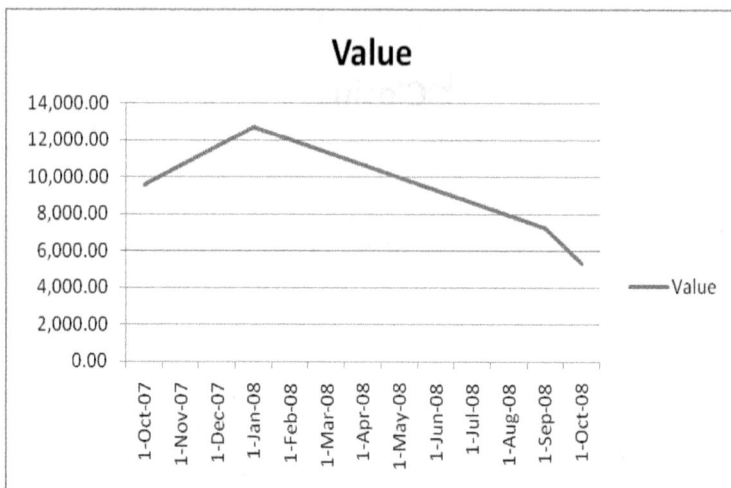

Value

Banking Industry

Banking in India has its origin as early as the Vedic period. It is believed that the transition from money lending to banking must have occurred even before Manu, the great Hindu Jurist, who has devoted a section of his work to deposits and advances and laid down rules relating to rates of interest. During the Mogul period, the indigenous bankers played a very important role in lending money and financing foreign trade and commerce. During the days of the East India Company, it was the turn of the agency houses to carry on the banking business.

The General Bank of India was the first Joint Stock Bank to be established in the year 1786. The others which followed were the Bank of Hindustan and the Bengal Bank. The Bank of Hindustan is reported to have continued till 1906 while the other two failed in the meantime. In the first half of the 19th century the East India Company established three banks; the Bank of Bengal in 1809, the Bank of Bombay in 1840 and the Bank of Madras in 1843. These three banks also known as Presidency Banks were independent units and functioned well. These three banks were amalgamated in 1920 and a new bank, the Imperial Bank of India was established on 27th January 1921.

With the passing of the State Bank of India Act in 1955 the undertaking of the Imperial Bank of India was taken over by the newly constituted State Bank of India. The Reserve Bank which is the Central Bank was created in 1935 by passing Reserve Bank of India Act 1934. In the wake of the Swadeshi Movement, a number of banks with Indian management were established in the country namely, Punjab National Bank Ltd, Bank of India Ltd, Canara Bank Ltd, Indian Bank Ltd, the Bank of Baroda Ltd, the Central Bank of India Ltd. On July 19, 1969, 14 major banks of the country were nationalized and in 15th April 1980 six more commercial private sector banks were also taken over by the government.

Today the commercial banking system in India can be broadly classified into the following sectors respectively;

- ❖ Schedule Commercial Bank
- ❖ Unschedule Commercial Bank

Schedule Commercial Bank:
Scheduled Commercial Banks Constitute those banks which have been included in the second schedule of Reserve Bank of India 1934. RBI in turn includes only those banks in

this schedule which satisfy the criteria laid down vide section 42. Scheduled banks constitute of commercial banks and co-operative banks. There are about 67,000 branches of Scheduled banks spread across India. As far as the present scenario is concerned the Banking Industry in India is going through a transitional phase This sub sector can Broadly be classified into:

- Public Sector Banks
- Private sectors Bank
- Co-operative Banks
- Foreign Banks.

Public Sector Bank

Which are the bases of the Banking sector in India account for more than 78 per cent of the total banking industry assets. Unfortunately they are burdened with excessive Non Performing assets (NPAs), massive manpower and lack of modern technology.

Public Sector bank have either the government of India as the majority shareholder. This segment comprises of State Bank of India (SBI) and its Subsidiaries (State Bank of Rajasthan, State bank of Bikaner and Jaipur) and Other Nationalized Bank (United Bank of India, Allah bad Bank, Bank of Borada (BOB), Punjab National Bank, Bank of India etc.

Private Sector Bank

The Private Sector Banks are making tremendous progress. They are leaders in Internet banking, mobile banking, phone banking, ATMs. Private Sector Banks operating are ING

Vyasa Bank, ICICI Bank, HDFC Bank, Axis Bank, IDBI Bank etc.

Co-operative Banks

These banks are formed on the principles of Co-operation. These banks extend credit facilities to Farmer and Small scale industrial concern.

Co-operative Banks operating are Surat peoples Co-operative Bank, Sarvoday Co-oprative Bank, The Surat Districts Co-operative Bank, City Co-opertative Bank, Prime Co-operative Bank, Mehasana Co-operative Banks, Varcha Co-opearative Bank etc.

Foreign Banks

As far as foreign banks are concerned they are likely to succeed in the Indian Banking Industry. These bank are type of commercial bank whose main function in financing of foreign trade. A few examples of such banks are Hong Kong Bank, Standard Charted Bank, City Bank, Bank of America etc.

Unscheduled Bank:

Unscheduled Commercial banks are those, which were not included in the second scheduled of the RBI Act 1934.

Industrial Bank

These banks are expected to provide long term financial assistance to industrial concerns. In our country, industrial banks are in form of specialized financial institutions

1. IFCI(Industrial Finance Corporation of India)
2. SFC(State Financial Corporation)
3. IDBI(Industrial Development Bank of India)

Agriculture Bank

These banks are established to meet the financial requirement of the farming class. These banks provide loans to the farmers at a low rate of interest. For Example NABARD

EXIM Bank

The Export- import bank was established in India on 1st January 1982 with the object of solving problem encountered by exporters in India. This bank pays special attention to the export of capital goods.

❖ **Recent Trend in Banking**

The growth in the Indian Banking Industry has been more qualitative than quantitative and it is expected to remain the same in the coming years. Based on the projections made in the "India Vision 2020" prepared by the Planning Commission and the Draft 10th Plan, the report forecasts that the pace of expansion in the balance-sheets of banks is likely to decelerate. The total asset of all scheduled commercial banks by end-March 2010 is estimated at Rs 40, 90,000 cores. That will comprise about 65 per cent of GDP at current market prices as compared to 67 per cent in 2002-03. Bank assets are expected to grow at an annual composite rate of 13.4 per cent during the rest of the decade as against the growth rate of 16.7 per cent that existed between 1994-95 and 2002-03. It is expected that there will be large additions to the capital base and reserves on the liability side.

❖ **Banking Sector in Budget 2008**

- The policies and initiatives taken in the Union Budget of India 2008-2009 on the Indian Banking sector were in tandem with the requirements of the Indian economy.

- Small and marginal farmers have been relieved of all farm loans, disbursed till March 2007 and also all loans, which are due till December 2007 and was unpaid till February 2008. These farm loan waivers would be facilitated by all the concerned Public Sector Banks and Regional Rural Banks of India. A total of Rs 60,000 cores would be waived-off under such scheme. The settlement of these loan-waivers will be offered through special type of scheme. Further, the Public Sector Banks and Regional Rural Banks of India were also suggested, to bring within their fold, a minimum of 250 rural household accounts at every branch every year.

- The Indira Awas Yojana was brought under the ambit of Public Sector Banks. Loan limit up to Rs 20,000 per unit at 4% interest was fixed under differential rate of interest (DRI) scheme. The Finance Minister also advised the Indian PSU Banks to open 288 branches in minority districts of India. Further, he also asked the Indian banking industry to embrace total financial inclusion. In another landmark decision, the Finance Minister, Mr. P. Chidambaram said that the Ex-banking servicemen in India would be offered employment opportunities in the banking sector.

- Another major announcement was that, the much talked-about 'Banking Cash Transaction Tax (BCTT)' would be withdrawn from the financial year 2009-2010. Experts believe the impact of the decisions and policies taken during the Union Budget of India 2008-2009 on the Indian Banking sector would be mixed. It is expected that the Indian PSU banks will face pressure on their net interest margins due to the waiving-off of agricultural loans. Further, the cumulative cost that will be incurred for opening up of new Regional Rural Banks in India may substantially increase the operating cost for the banks. The inclusion of the Indira Awas Yojana houses under the differential rate of interest scheme and at 4% interest will increase the proportion of sub-PLR lending for the concerned banks.

- The major Public Sector Banks of India like the State Bank of India, Bank of Baroda, Punjab National Bank may see their net interest margins shrinking till the subsidy for waiver of agricultural loans is being completely released. Moreover, experts are skeptical about the long term benefit of such agricultural loan waiver as offered through the Union Budget of India 2008-2009.

4. Banks Profile

SBI Bank

The SBI's powerful corporate banking formation deploys multiple channels to deliver integrated solutions for all financial challenges faced by the corporate universe. The Corporate Banking Group and the National Banking Group are the primary delivery channels for corporate banking products. It was nationalized and reconstituted in 1955.

The Corporate Banking Group consists of dedicated Strategic Business Units that cater exclusively to specific client groups or specialize in particular product clusters. Foremost among these a specialized group is the Corporate Accounts Group (CAG), focusing on the prime corporate and institutional clients of the country's biggest business centers. The others are the Project Finance unit and the Leasing unit. The National Banking Group also delivers the entire spectrum of corporate banking products to other corporate clients, on a nationwide platform.

Registered Office	State Bank Bhavan 8th Floor Madame Cama Marg, Mumbai Maharashtra 400021.	BSE Code	500112
Tel:	22883888,,,	NSE Code	SBINEQ
Fax	22855348,	Face Value	10
Email	cgmac@mumbai.coborn.sb	Market	1

	i.co.in	Lot	
Website	www.sbi.co.in , www.statebankofindia.com		
Business Group	SBI Group		
Industry	Finance - Banks - Public Sector		

HDFC Bank

The Housing Development Finance Corporation Limited (HDFC) was amongst the first to receive an 'in-principle' approval from the Reserve Bank of India (RBI) to set up a bank in the private sector, as part of the RBI's liberalisation of the Indian Banking Industry in 1994. The bank was incorporated in August 1994 in the name of 'HDFC Bank Limited', with its registered office in Mumbai, India. HDFC Bank commenced operations as a Scheduled Commercial Bank in January 1995.

HDFC Bank, India's premier private sector bank, promoted by HDFC Group, has established a strong presence in both retail and corporate finance. The bank also has active treasury and capital market operations. The bank has a wide reach across the country with a branch network of 404 branches and 900 ATMs. It is acknowledged as one of the most efficient private sector banks in the country. HDFC Bank is also a pioneer of the retail-banking movement in India. It is one of the fastest growing and most profitable banks in India with a strong urban presence. Strong understanding of the retail sphere and inorganic growth initiatives have made it the second largest private sector bank in the count Currently , HDFC Bank has 550+ branches located in 240 cities of India, and all branches of the bank are linked on an online real-time basis. The bank offers many innovative products & services to individuals, corporates, trusts, governnments, partnerships, financial institutions, mutual funds, insurance companies. The bank also has over 1300 ATMs. In the next few month the number of branches and ATMs should go up substantially.

Registered Office	Ramon House , 5th Floor, 169, Back bay Reclamation Churchgate Mumbai Maharashtra 400020.	BSE Code	500180
Tel:	22850032,,,	NSE Code	HDFCBANKEQ
Fax	22046758-22046834,	Face Value	10
Email	-	Market Lot	1
Website	www.hdfcbank.com		
Business Group	HDFC Group		
Industry	Finance - Banks - Private Sector		

ICICI Bank

ICICI Bank is India's second-largest bank. The Bank has a network of about 573 branches and extension counters and over 2,000 ATMs. ICICI Bank was originally promoted in 1994 by ICICI Limited, an Indian financial institution, and was its wholly-owned subsidiary.ICICI was formed in 1955 at the initiative of the World Bank, the Government of India and representatives of Indian industry. The objective was to create a development financial institution for providing medium-term and long-term project financing to Indian businesses.

In the 1990s, ICICI transformed its business from a development financial institution offering only project finance to a diversified financial services group offering a wide variety of products and services, both directly and through a number of subsidiaries and affiliates like ICICI Bank. In 1999, ICICI become the first Indian company and the first bank or financial institution from non-Japan Asia to be listed on the NYSE. In 2001, ICICI bank acquired Bank of Madura Limited.

ICICI Bank set up its international banking group in fiscal 2002 to cater to the cross border needs of clients and leverage on its domestic banking strengths to offer products internationally. ICICI Bank currently has subsidiaries in the United Kingdom, Canada and Russia, branches in Singapore and Bahrain and representative offices in the United States, China, United Arab Emirates, Bangladesh and South Africa.

Today, ICICI Bank offers a wide range of banking products and financial services to corporate and retail customers through a variety of delivery channels and through its specialized subsidiaries and affiliates in the areas of investment banking, life and non-life insurance, venture capital and asset management.

Registered Office	"Landmark', Race Course Circle, Alkapuri Vadodra Gujarat 390007	BSE Code	532174
Tel:	339923,339924,339925,	NSE Code	ICICIBANKEQ
Fax	339926,	Face Value	10
Email	info@icicibank.com	Market Lot	1
Website	http://www.icicibank.com		
CEO	Mr.K V Kamath		
Business Group	ICICI Group		
Industry	Finance - Banks - Private Sector		

Bank of Baroda

Bank of Baroda (BSE: 532134) is a bank in India established on July 20, 1908 in the princely state of Baroda, in Gujarat. The bank, along with 13 other major commercial banks of India, was nationalisd on 19th July, 1969, by the Government of India.

In its international expansion Bank of Baroda followed the Indian diaspora, and especially that of the Gujaratis. Bank of

Baroda has total assets of about Rs.1133bn (end-Mar 2006), a network of over 2800 branches and offices, and about 700 ATMs. Bank of Baroda offers a wide range of banking products and financial services to corporate and retail customers through a variety of delivery channels and through its specialised subsidiaries and affiliates in the areas of investment banking, credit cards and asset management. Bank Of Baroda is the fifth largest bank in India with business crossing Rs. 1.78 lakh crores.

Registered Office	Bank of Baroda, Baroda Corporate Centre, Plot No - C-26, G - Block, Bandra Kurla Complex, Mumbai India	BSE Code	532134
Tel:	26102303,26196487,,	NSE Code	-
Fax	26108741,	Face Value	10
Email	ipo@bobindia.com	Market Lot	1
WebSite	www.bankofbaroda.com		
Chairman	Anil K. Khandelwal		
Business Group	Public Sector		

5. Analysis

A. Fundamental

Fundamental analysis is the examination of the underlying forces that affect the well being of the economy, industry groups, and companies. As with most analysis, the goal is to derive a forecast and profit from future price movements. At the company level, fundamental analysis may involve examination of financial data, management, business concept and competition, at the industry level, there might be an examination of supply and demand forces for the products offered. For the national economy, fundamental analysis might focus on economic data to assess the present and future growth of the economy. To forecast future stock prices, fundamental analysis combines economic, industry and company analysis to derive a stock's current fair value and forecast future value. If fair value is not equal to the current stock price, fundamental analysts believe that the stock is either over or under valued and the market price will ultimately gravitate towards fair value. Fundamentalists do not heed the advice of the random walkers and believe that markets are weak form efficient. By believing that prices do not accurately reflect all available information, fundamental analysts try to capitalize on perceived price discrepancies.

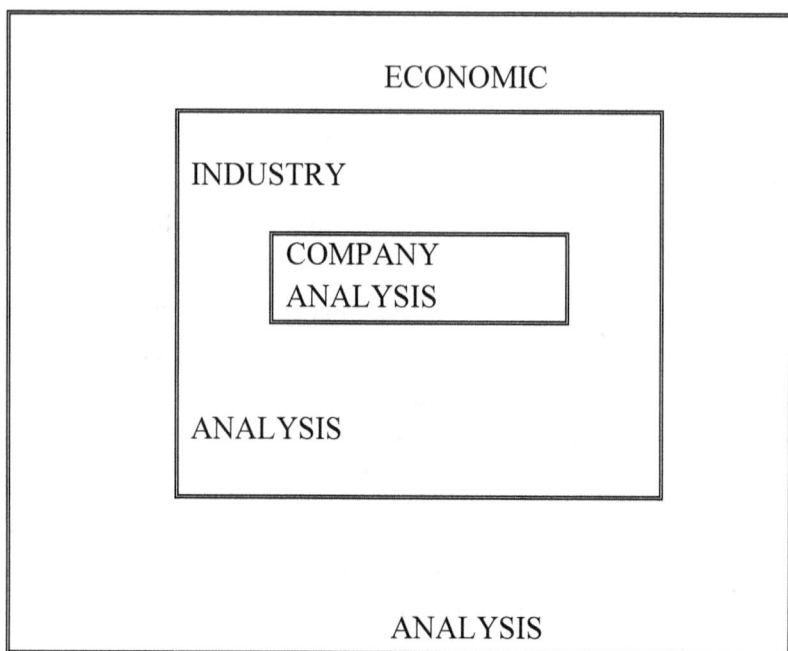

```
┌─────────────────────────────────────────────┐
│              ECONOMIC                         │
│   ┌─────────────────────────────────────┐    │
│   │ INDUSTRY                             │    │
│   │        ┌──────────────────┐         │    │
│   │        │ COMPANY          │         │    │
│   │        │ ANALYSIS         │         │    │
│   │        └──────────────────┘         │    │
│   │                                     │    │
│   │   ANALYSIS                          │    │
│   │                                     │    │
│   └─────────────────────────────────────┘    │
│                                               │
│              ANALYSIS                         │
└─────────────────────────────────────────────┘
```

B.   Economic

If the economy of the country booming, Income are rising very rapidly and also increase in demands of different products so, ultimately industry & companies may prosper.

There are different faces in business cycles & causing for movement in the economy each as, boom, depression, recession, recovery, peak point etc. The performance of the economy ultimately affect to the performance of the different industries & different companies. It ultimately affect to the price of securities.

Economic Scenario

With the central government's budget for FY 2007-08 all around economic indictor show a vibrant economy. Inflation is going up to 6.68%. After that the Rate of inflation in India rich top high in previous years. Now the rate of inflation is 11.80%. The currency of India (Rs.) is decreases vis-à-vis the American currency ($). Export & import are rising continuously and also substantially increasing in foreign reserved India.

Following are the indicators of the economy of the country

1) GDP(Gross Domestic Product)
2) Inflation (WPI weekly)
3) Exchange Rate
4) Foreign Direct Investment

According to economic analysis we can judge our country India financial situation and also judge various industry sector present conditions in market. I can also judge through economic analysis present condition of banking sector.

GDP (Gross Domestic Product)

The estimate of real GDP for FY 2007-08 & Current year 2008-09 is place [As per estimation of central statistical organization].

Year	GDP rate
2000-01	4.40%
2001-02	5.80%
2002-03	3.80%
2003-04	8.50%
2004-05	6.90%

2005-06	8.10%
2006-07	9.20%
2007-08	8.50%
2008-09 (April to Sep-2008)	7.90%

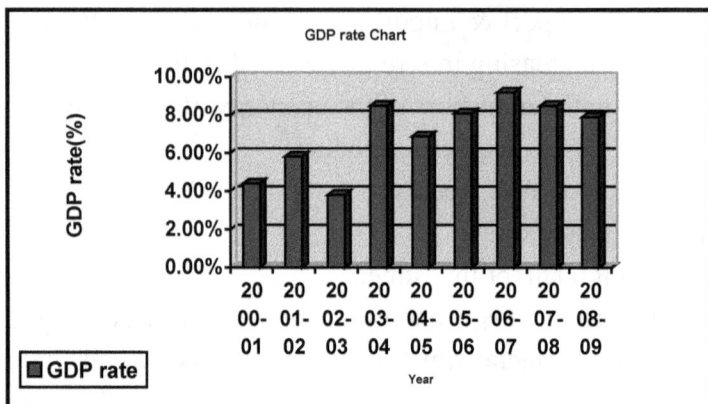

GDP rate Chart

Performance of Industry Sector

For the first time in the last 10 years, industrial's GDP rate growth in India has exceeded 10 per cent.

Year	GDP rate
2000-01	6.50%
2001-02	3.60%
2002-03	6.60%
2003-04	6.70%
2004-05	7.80%

2005-06	8.30%
2006-07	10.60%
2007-08	8.40%

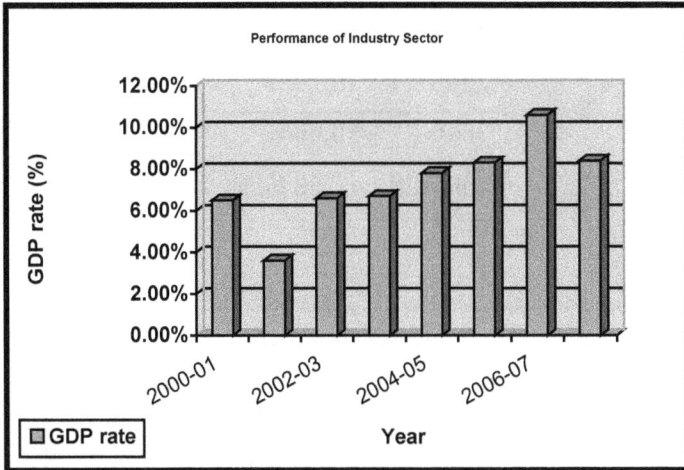

Performance of Service Sector

India's services sector has grown very fast as it holds a larger portion of young peoples. The educated young masses in India have brought tremendous success for the country in the recent years. The services sector in the country has benefited from the availability of vast skilled labor. There is need to improve the availability of educational facilities at all levels – primary, secondary and tertiary – to equip the labor with the necessary skills to maintain current competitive advantage.

Year	GDP rate
2000-01	5.50%
2001-02	6.80%
2002-03	7.90%
2003-04	9.10%
2004-05	8.90%
2005-06	10.20%
2006-07	10.60%
2007-08	10.50%

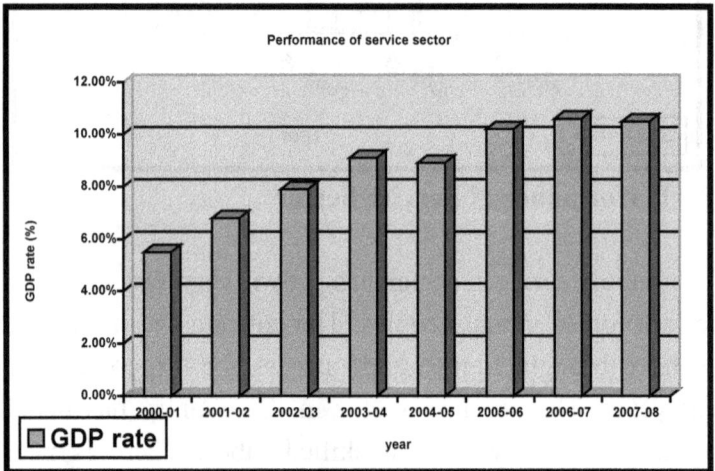

Performance of service sector

Inflation Rate

Inflation rate continuously increase on comparison of preceding year.

Date	Inflation Rate (%)
10 Aug 2004	7.51
24 Oct 2006	5.16
1 March 2007	6
17 May 2007	5.66
24 August 2007	4.05
15 March 2008	5.11
28 March 2008	6.68
2 May 2008	7.57
30 May 2008	8.1
19 June 2008	11.02
27 June 2008	11.42
30 Aug 2008	12.36
25 Sep 2008	12.14
3 Oct 2008	11.99
10 Oct 2008	11.80
18 Oct 2008	11.44

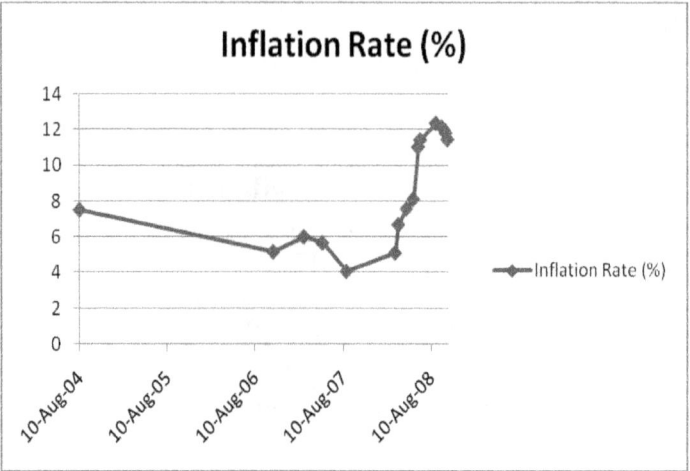

Inflation Rate (%)

FDI (Foreign Direct Investment)

FDI	Us $ million
2001-02	6130
2002-03	5035
2003-04	4322
2004-05	6051
2005-06	7722
2006-07	22079
2007-08	29893
2008-09	10073

FDI

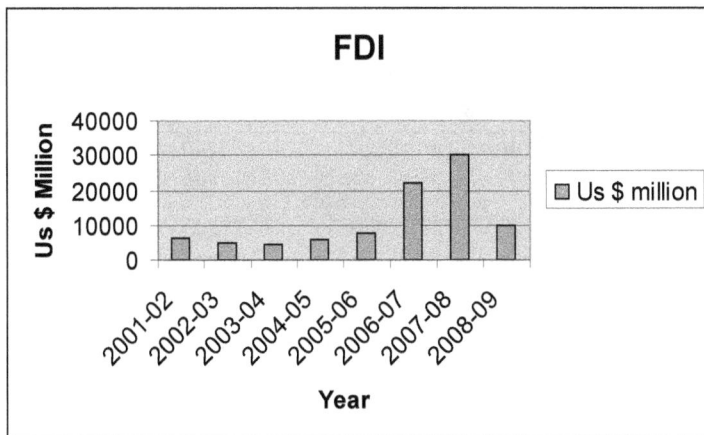

Exchange Rate

The US dollar stands as the world's currency of choice. There are a few currencies that are more valuable than dollar in exchange Term, however the dollar remain the chosen currency for global trade and measurement of almost all the economic metrics.

Date	Rs. Vs $
30 Sep 2007	40.1735
31 Oct 2007	39.3661
30 Nov 2007	39.3267
31 Dec 2007	39.3750
31 Jan 2008	39.2676
28 Feb 2008	39.6735
31 March 2008	40.1452
30th April 2008	39.9668
31st May 2008	42.0019
30th June 2008	42.7633

31st July 2008	42.7027
31st August 2008	42.9057
30th September 2008	47.425
4th October 2008	47.067

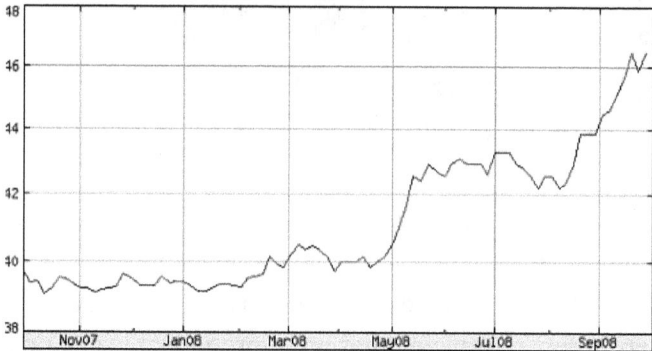

From above chart I can say that Indian currency is continuously being Weak against US $ from the May 2008 to the till date and before May 2008 Indian Rs. Strong against US$.

C.   Industry

The identification of environmental issues is helpful in structuring environmental appraisal so that the strategists have a good idea of where the environmental opportunities and threats lie. Structuring the environmental appraisal is a difficult process as environmental issues do not lend themselves to a straightforward classification.

Issues may arise simultaneously from more than one sector of the environment. Strategists have to use their experience and judgment to place the different environmental issues where they mainly belong so that clarity can emerge.

There are many techniques available to structure the environmental appraisal. One of the techniques, suggested by Glueck, is that of preparing an Environmental Threat and Opportunity Profile (ETOP) for an organization.

The preparation of ETOP involves dividing the environment into different sectors and then analyzing the impact of each sector on the organization. A comprehensive ETOP requires subdividing each environmental sector into sub-factors and then the impact of each sub-factor on the organization is described in the form of a statement.

However, there can be some environmental factors which may cause no impact on the industry at all as that industry of sector may be water tight in its nature form those sector or may be not at all related to those factors, such sectors are marked by a horizontal double pointed arrow ($\leftrightarrow$). In case some factor is causing a positive impact then it is pointed by an upward arrow ($\uparrow$) and a negative impact making factor with a downward arrow ($\downarrow$).

Following the same concept, in order to understand which sector is better for the investment, an ETOP study can be conducted of the various sectors and hence an analysis can be done as to understand which sector is the best, keeping in mind the future prospects.

To take a look at the '**Banking Sector**' the various factors affecting it and causing a sizable impact on it are;

ETOP of Banking Sector/Industry		
Environmental Factor	**Nature of Impact**	**Description**
1. Market (Micro Env.)	↑	- Huge rise in Banking sector's Q3 Income.
	↑	- Banks going for M&A's heavily to expand their market.
2. Economic, Political & Governmental.	↑	* - Banking and securities Act (BSA) launched by the Government has heavily reduced the NPA's or Default customers of the banks.
	↓	- Banks may loose a large part of their profits when interest rates rise due to sinking treasury income.
	↑	- Banks may get to invest 10% of their deposits in stocks (previously only 5% was allowed).
	↑	- Banks and MF's may soon be allowed to trade in Commodity futures (5-10% of advances).
	↑	- Government stays firm on its decision to hold more then 51% shares of PSU banks.

	↓	- RBI guides banks M&A to get Tax-breaks.
	↓	- Banks fear excessive control by Government.
3. Socio-Cultural	↔	- No significant threat or affect assumed from this factor.
4. Technological	↔	- No significant threat or affect assumed from this factor.
5. Demographic	↔	- No significant threat or affect assumed from this factor.
6. Natural	↔	- No significant threat or affect assumed from this factor.
7. International	↓	- Foreign banks may be allowed to creep up 10% a year in Pvt. Banks.
* - Such fields have no solid base but are believed in general by everyone.		

To talk about the banking sector, one of the leading sectors of the year 2008 was the banking sector. This was proved by the increasing Quarter incomes of the banks (Q3). Along-with, the heavy M&A's taking place, the permission given by the government to banks to invest in stocks and commodities & the government's decision to hold more the 51% of its stakes of PSU's also helped. But at the same time the banks now also fear of increasing interest rates of RBI & increasing power of the government to control banks.

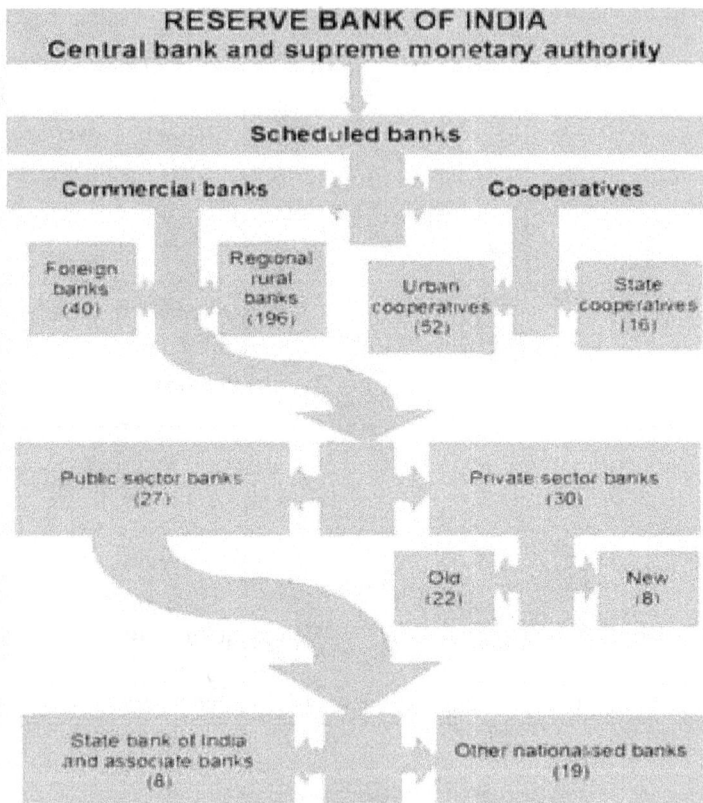

RESERVE BANK OF INDIA
Central bank and supreme monetary authority

Scheduled banks

Commercial banks

Co-operatives

Foreign banks (40)

Regional rural banks (196)

Urban cooperatives (52)

State cooperatives (16)

Public sector banks (27)

Private sector banks (30)

Old (22)

New (8)

State bank of India and associate banks (8)

Other nationalised banks (19)

Structure of the organised banking sector in India. Numbers of banks are in brackets.

Market Capitalizations of Bank
(as on 8 Sep 2008)

Bank	Market Cap.(Rs. in crore)
SBI	101044.33
ICICI Bank	80233.17
HDFC Bank	55271.47
Bank of Baroda	11022.85

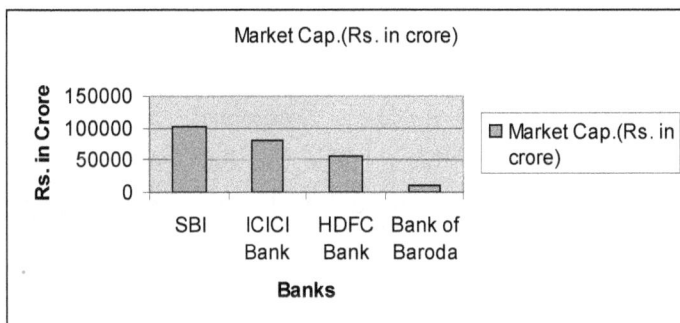

Market Cap.(Rs. in crore)

Asset Size of Bank (Rs.in crore)

Bank	Total Assest
SBI	722,125.08
ICICI Bank	400417.12
Bank of Baroda	179,599.52
HDFC Bank	133,251.01

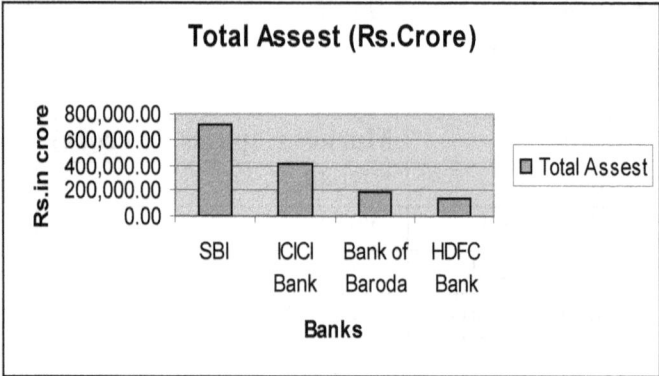

Total Asset (Rs.Crore)

D.   Company Analysis

Ratio analysis is a powerful tool of financial analysis. A ratio is defined as "the indicated quotient of two mathematical expressions" and as "the relationship between two or more things." A ratio is used as a benchmark for evaluating the financial position and performance of a firm.

The absolute accounting figures reported in the financial statements do not provide a meaningful understanding of the performance and financial position of a firm. An accounting figure conveys meaning when it is related to some other relevant information. For example, a Rs 5 crore net profit may look impressive, but the firm's performance can be said to be good or bad only when the net profit figure is related to the firm's investment. The relationship between two accounting figures, expressed mathematically, is known as a financial ratio (or simply as a ratio). Ratios help to summarize large quantities of financial data and to make qualitative judgment about the firm's financial performance.

Several ratios, calculated from the accounting data, can be grouped into various classes according to financial activity or function to be evaluated. In view of the requirements of the various users of ratios, we may classify them into the following four important categories:

1. Liquidity ratios
2. Leverage ratios
3. Activity ratios
4. Profitability ratios.

❖ **Liquidity Ratios:** Liquidity ratios measure the firm's ability to meet current obligations; leverage ratios show the proportions of debt and equity in financing the firm's assets; activity ratios reflect the firm's efficiency in utilizing its assets, and profitability ratios measure overall performance and effectiveness of the firm.

❖ **Leverage Ratios:** To judge the long-term financial position of the firm, financial leverage, or capital structure, ratios are calculated. These ratios indicate mix of funds provided by owners and lenders. As a general rule, there should be an appropriate mix of debt and owners' equity in financing the firm's assets.

❖ **Activity Ratios:** Activity ratios are employed to evaluate the efficiency with which the firm manages and utilizes its assets. These ratios are also known as turnover ratios because they indicate the speed with which assets are being converted or turned over into sales. Activity ratios, thus, involve a relationship between sales and assets.

ଔ **Profitability Ratios:** The profitability ratios are calculated to measure the operating efficiency of the company. Besides management of the company, creditors and owners are also interested in the profitability of the firm.

Some of the most important and most frequently types of ratios are discussed below and are hence also utilized in the project further.

1. Current ratio
2. Gross Profit ratio
3. Net Profit ratio
4. Return on Equity ratio
5. Return on Assets
6. Earnings per Share
7. Dividends per Share
8. Price Earnings Ratio (P/E Ratio)
9. Book Value

Current Ratio:

The current ratio is calculated by dividing current assets by current liabilities:

Current Ratio = Total Current Assets / Total Current Liabilities.

The current ratio is a measure of the firm's short-term solvency. It indicates the availability of current assets in rupees for every one rupee of current liability. A ratio of greater than one means that the firm has more current assets than current claims against them. As a conventional rule, a current ratio of 2:1 or more is considered satisfactory.

	Current Ratio			
	SBI	ICICI	BOB	HDFC
March-2008	0.5361	0.48	0.34	0.27
March-2007	0.4235	0.44	0.62	0.2756
Average	0.48	0.46	0.47	0.2728
Rank	1	3	2	4

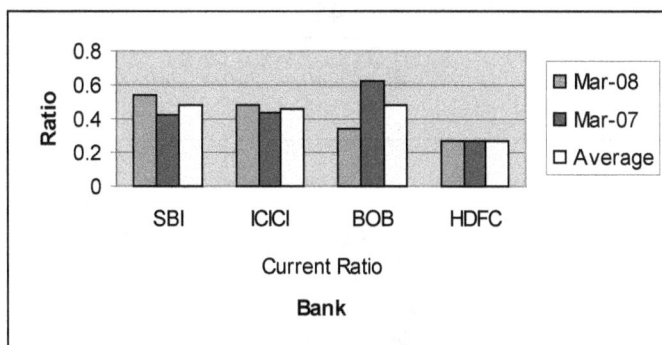

Interpretation:

The current ratio indicates the current position of the business. The two year average current ratios of SBI bank & BoB have higher than other bank. Current year current ratios SBI have higher than other bank.

Earnings per Share:

This is, perhaps, the fundamental investor ratio: in this case, we work out the average amount of profits earned per ordinary share issued. EPS calculations made over years indicate whether or not the firm's earnings power on per-share basis has changed over that period. The formula is:

EPS = Profit after Tax / Number of Common Shares Outstanding.

	EARNINGS PER SHARE(Rs)			
	SBI	**ICICI**	**BOB**	**HDFC**
March-2008	103.94	36.02	37.92	43.42
March-2007	83.91	32.88	27.15	34.55
Average	93.925	34.45	32.535	38.985
Rank	1	3	4	2

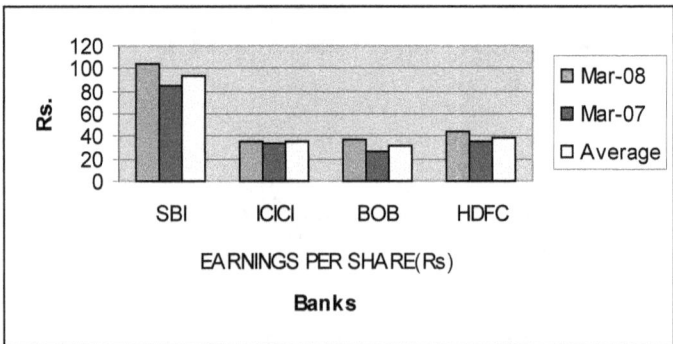

Interpretation:

This ratio measures the profit available to the equity share holder on a per share basis this is the amount that they can get on every shareholder. The average of two year of SBI given highest EPS (93.925)

Return on Equity:

It determines the rate of return on your investment in the business. As an owner or shareholder this is one of the most important ratios as it shows the hard fact about the business -- are you making enough of a profit to compensate you for the risk of being in business.

ROE Ratio = Net Profit / Total Equity.

	RETURN ON EQUITY RATIO (%)			
	SBI	**ICICI**	**BOB**	**HDFC**
March-2008	16.75	11.75	14.58	17.74
March-2007	15.45	13.37	12.45	19.46
Average	16.1	12.56	13.515	18.6
Rank	2	4	3	1

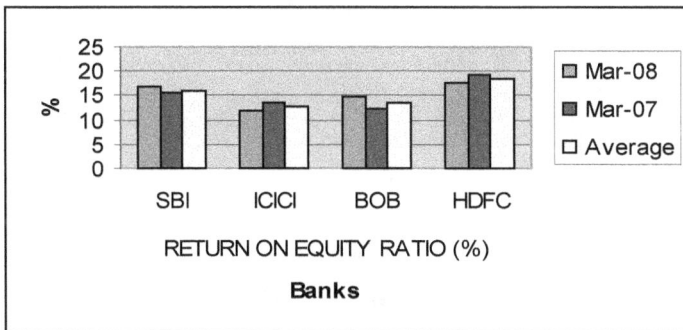

Interpretation:

The return on equity tells us what has been the return on the total capital that was invested by the shareholders of the firm. In this ratio HDFC return on equity average of 2 year is 18.6% higher than other Banks.

Book Value:

	Book Value in Rs.			
	SBI	**ICICI**	**BOB**	**HDFC**
March-2008	776.48	417.64	302.13	324.39
March-2007	594.69	270.35	236.64	201.42
Average	685.585	343.99	269.38	262.90
Rank	1	2	3	4

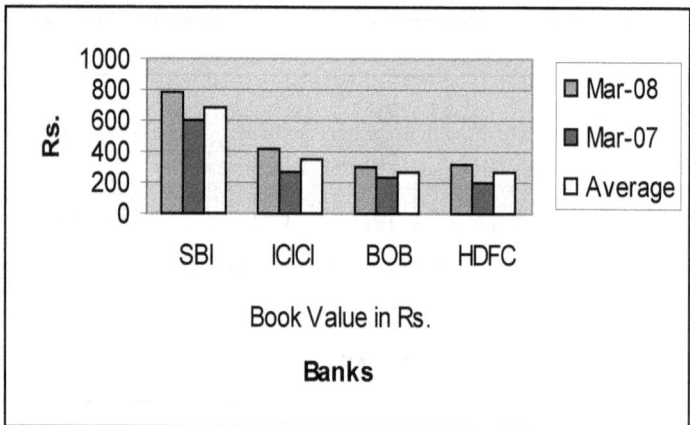

Interpretation:

This ratio indicates the current book value of the company in the market. The average of two year SBI has highest

book value Rs. 685.585. Current year SBI has highest book value Rs. 776.48.

Price Earnings Ratio:

The P/E ratio is a vital ratio for investors. Basically, it gives us an indication of the confidence that investors have in the future prosperity of the business. A P/E ratio of 1 shows very little confidence in that business whereas a P/E ratio of 20 expresses a great deal of optimism about the future of a business. Its calculation is as follows:

P/E Ratio = Current Market Share Price / Earning per Share

	P/E Ratio(Rs.)			
	SBI	**ICICI**	**BOB**	**HDFC**
March-2008	15.38	21.38	7.49	30.40
Rank	3	2	4	1

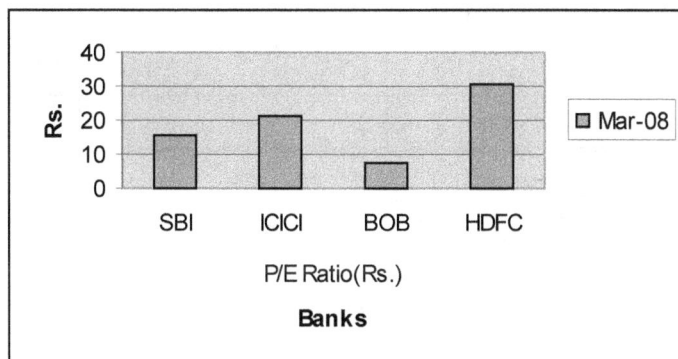

Interpretation:

The price earnings ratio tells us about the future prospect of the companies, i.e. whether people are expecting the company's share prices to go up or down. Now a day HDFC Bank price earning ratio is higher than other banks (30.40).

Dividend Per share:

The net profits after taxes belong to shareholders. But the income which they really receive is the amount of earnings distributed as cash dividends. Therefore, a large number of present and potential investors may be interested in DPS, rather than EPS. Its calculation is as follows:

DPS = Dividends / Number of Ordinary Shares Outstanding

	Dividend Per Share			
	SBI	ICICI	BOB	HDFC
March-2008	21.5	11.00	8.0	8.5
March-2007	14.00	10.00	6.0	7.0
Average	17.75	10.5	7.0	7.75
Rank	1	2	4	3

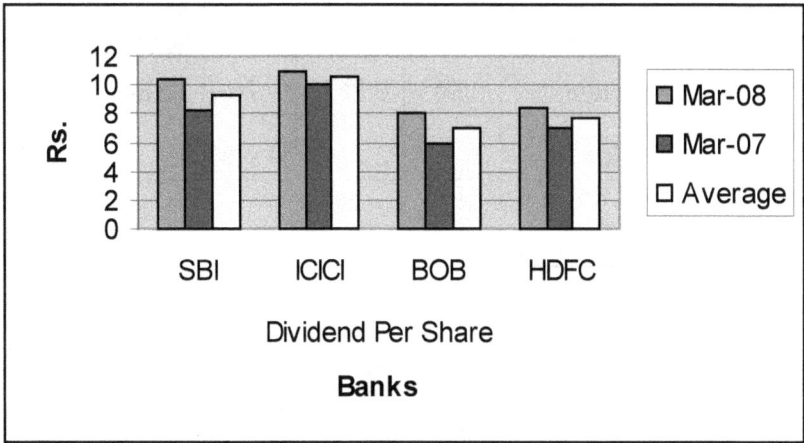

Dividend Per Share

Banks

Interpretation:

The term that provides a direct impact on the investors is the dividends provided by the company to its investors. SBI Provide high dividend pay out ratio 21.75 & average 17.75.

Return on Assets:

This measures how efficiently profits are being generated from the assets employed in the business when compared with the ratios of firms in a similar business. A low ratio in comparison with industry averages indicates an inefficient use of business assets. The Return on Assets Ratio is calculated as follows:

ROA Ratio = Net Profit / Total Assets of the Firm.

	Return on Assets (%)			
	SBI	**ICICI**	**BOB**	**HDFC**
March-2008	0.93	1.03	0.80	1.119

March-2007	0.80	0.90	0.72	1.25
Average	0.865	0.965	0.76	1.1845
Rank	3	2	4	1

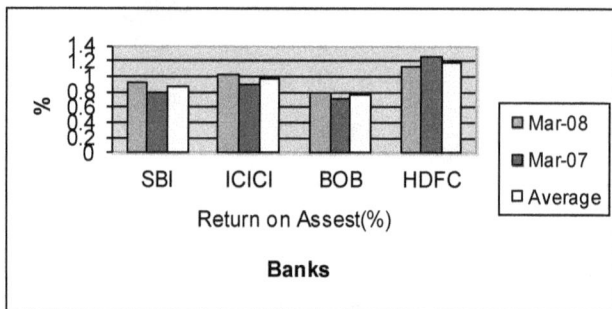

Interpretation:

Whether the firm has seen a justifiable growth in comparison to its assets holding, is what is displayed by this ratio. HDFC return on assets ratio average is 1.1845% higher than the other industry.

Net Profit Ratio:

This ratio is the percentage of sales dollars left after subtracting the Cost of Goods sold and all expenses, except income taxes. It provides a good opportunity to compare your company's "return on sales" with the performance of other companies in your industry. It is calculated before income tax because tax rates and tax liabilities vary from company to company for a wide variety of reasons, making comparisons after taxes much more difficult. The Net Profit Margin Ratio is calculated as follows:

NP Ratio = Net Profit / Net Sales.

	Net Profit Ratio (%)			
	SBI	**ICICI**	**BOB**	**HDFC**
March-2008	11.51	10.48	10.33	12.83
March-2007	10.17	10.74	9.83	13.84
Average	10.84	10.61	10.08	13.33
Rank	2	3	4	1

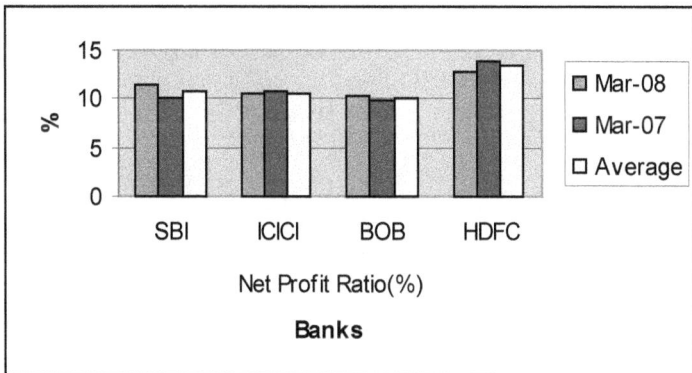

Interpretation:

A high net profit margin would ensure adequate return to the owner as well as enable a firm to withstand adverse economic condition when pricing is declining, cost of production is raising and demand of the product is falling. In this ratio also HDFC ratio is high.

Gross Profit Ratio:

This ratio is the percentage of sales dollars left after subtracting the cost of goods sold from net sales. It measures the percentage of sales dollars remaining (after obtaining or manufacturing the goods sold) available to pay the overhead expenses of the company. Comparison of your business ratios to those of similar businesses will reveal the relative strengths or weaknesses in your business.

GP Ratio = Gross Profit / Net Sales

	Gross Profit Ratio (%)			
	SBI	ICICI	BOB	HDFC
March-2008	66.15	69.68	67.21	52.24
March-2007	59.82	67.22	61.82	52.42
Average	62.98	68.45	64.51	52.33
Rank	3	1	2	4

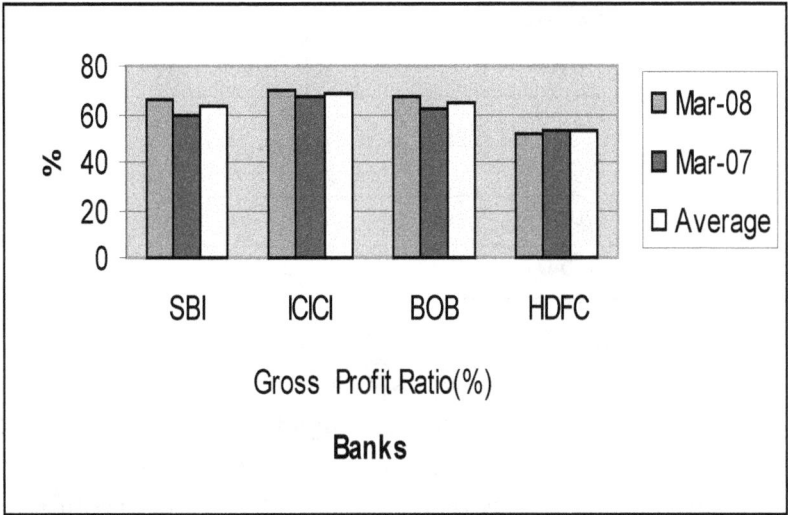

Gross Profit Ratio(%)

Banks

**Price History's
Bank of Baroda**

Month	Price
Oct 18 2008	304
Oct 16 2008	305
Sep 08	287.35
Aug 08	284.30
Jul 08	255.50
June 08	203.25
May 08	270.05
April 08	315.15

Mar 08	283.90
Feb 08	365.75
Jan 08	388.90
Dec 07	459.60
Nov 07	382.20
Oct 07	342.35
Sep 07	326.60

Interpretation:

Gross profit ratio is the result of relationship between prices, sales, volumes and costs. A high ratio of GP to sales is a sign of good management as it implies that the cost of production of the firm is relatively low. ICICI gross profit ratio is higher than other Banks..

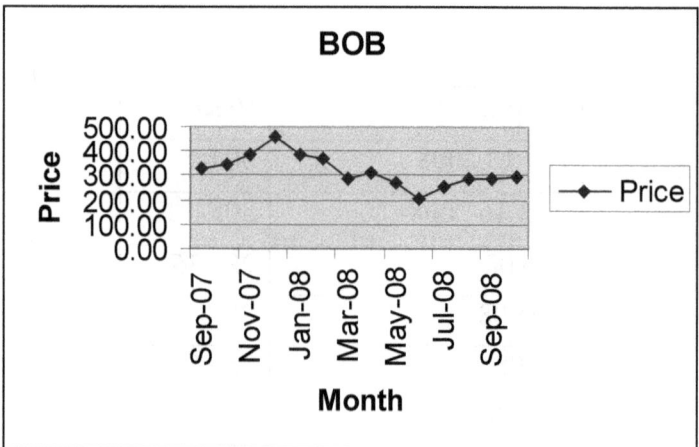

SBI Bank

Month	Price
18 Oct 08	1413
Oct 08(16 Oct)	1500
Sep 08€	1405
Aug 08	1,403.60
Jul 08	1,414.75
June 08	1,111.45
May 08	1,443.35
April 08	1,776.35
Mar 08	1,598.85
Feb 08	2,109.70
Jan 08	2,162.25
Dec 07	2,237.09
Nov 07	2,170.38
Oct 07	1,951.34
Sep 07	1,840.52

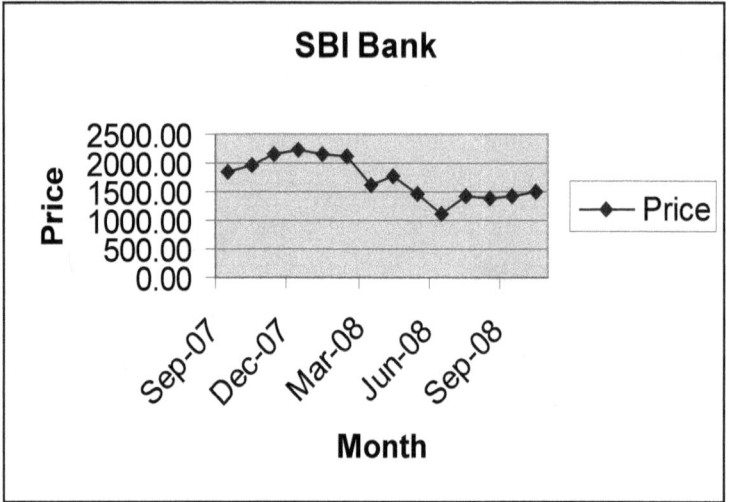

SBI Bank

ICICI Bank

Month	Price
18 Oct 08	391
Oct 08(16 Oct.)	414
Sep 08	493.30
Aug 08	671.50
Jul 08	634.85
June 08	630.20
May 08	788.30
April 08	879.40
Mar 08	770.10
Feb 08	1,090.95
Jan 08	1,145.65

Dec 07	1,232.40
Nov 07	1,184.65
Oct 07	1,257.00
Sep 07	1,063.15

ICICI Bank

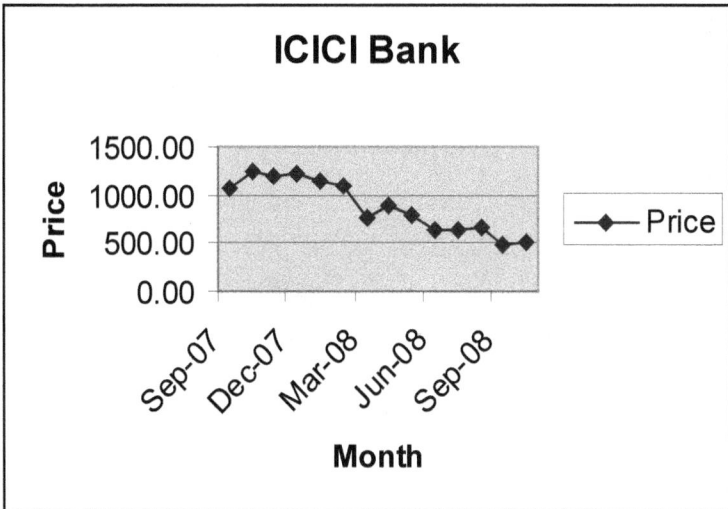

HDFC Bank

Month	Price
Oct 08(16 Oct)	1024..05
Sep 08	1199.50
Aug 08	1,277.25
Jul 08	1,095.25
June 08	1,002.30
May 08	1,357.85
April 08	1,514.85

Mar 08	1,319.95
Feb 08	1,453.45
Jan 08	1,568.00
Dec 07	1,727.80
Nov 07	1,719.00
Oct 07	1,653.10
Sep 07	1,439.05

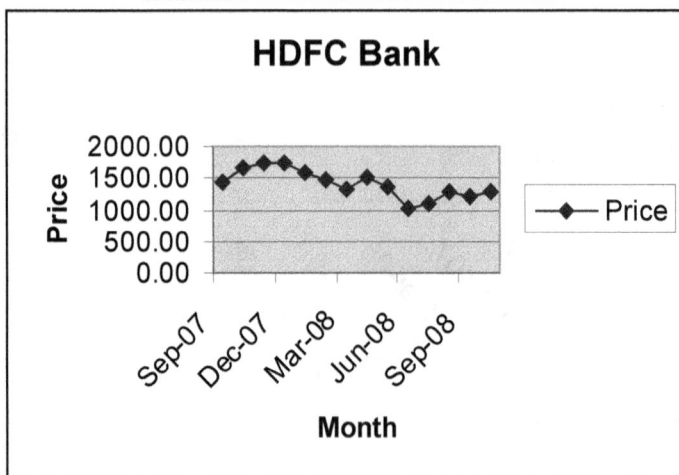

HDFC Bank

Shareholding Pattern

ICICI Bank

Shareholding	%
Foreign Holdings	68.31
Govt. / Financial Institutions	17.53
Corporate Bodies(not covered above)	6.49

| Directors and their Relatives | 0 |
| Other including Indian Public | 7.68 |

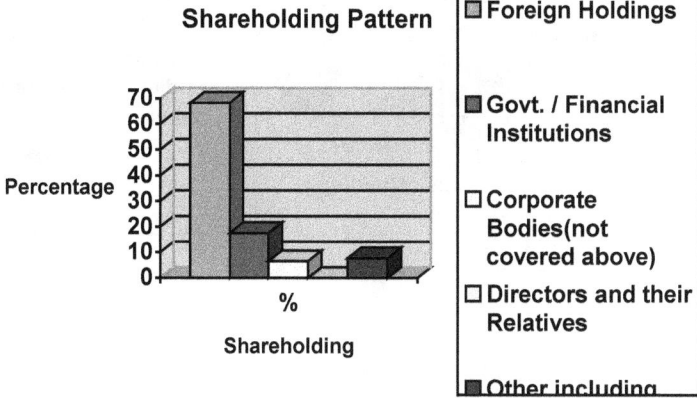

Shareholding Pattern

Legend:
- Foreign Holdings
- Govt. / Financial Institutions
- Corporate Bodies(not covered above)
- Directors and their Relatives
- Other including

SBI

Shareholding	%
Foreign Holdings	19.19
Govt. / Financial Institutions	11.55
Corporate Bodies(not covered above)	3.17
Directors and their Relatives	59.41
Other including Indian Public	6.64

Shareholding Pattern

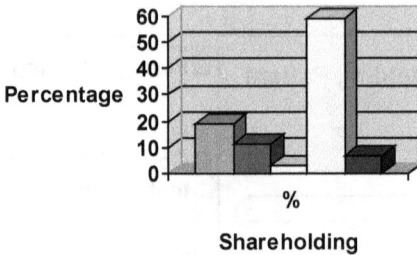

Percentage (60, 50, 40, 30, 20, 10, 0)

% Shareholding

Legend:
- Foreign Holdings
- Govt. / Financial Institutions
- Corporate Bodies(not covered above)
- Directors and their Relatives

BOB

Shareholding	%
Foreign Holdings	20.23
Govt. / Financial Institutions	17.68
Corporate Bodies(not covered above)	1.43
Directors and their Relatives	53.81
Other including Indian Public	6.84

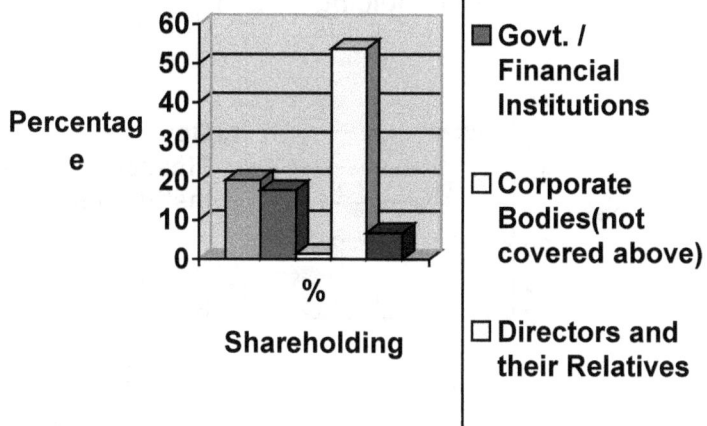

Shareholding Pattern

Percentage vs **% Shareholding**

Legend:
- Foreign Holdings
- Govt. / Financial Institutions
- Corporate Bodies(not covered above)
- Directors and their Relatives

HDFC

Shareholding	%
Foreign Holdings	50.90
Govt. / Financial Institutions	7.82
Corporate Bodies(not covered above)	10.01
Directors and their Relatives	19.42

Other including Indian Public	11.86

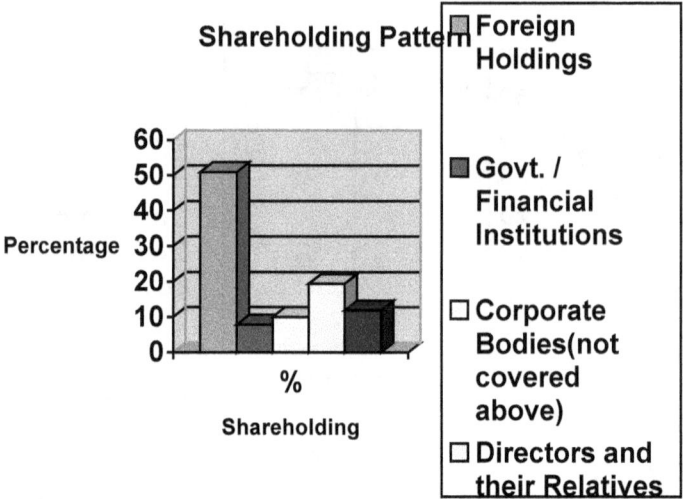

Shareholding Pattern

Percentage

60
50
40
30
20
10
0

%

Shareholding

- ☐ Foreign Holdings
- ■ Govt. / Financial Institutions
- ☐ Corporate Bodies(not covered above)
- ☐ Directors and their Relatives

6. FINDING

Todays global pass very tough situation because of global crisis. This matter affect of all industry sector of the world. India also not retain of this big Problem. India also not retain of this big Problem. Due to the global financial Crisis in India:

➢ The GDP rate is decrease
➢ Inflation rate is increase
➢ Indian Rupees weak against US $ and
➢ FDI is also decrease in India

From the fundamental analysis of four Bank (ICICI Bank, HDFC Bank, SBI Bank, Bank of Baroda), I have found that the performance and financial result of each bank are too much good also seen that SBI have better result compare to other bank. It does not mean that other banks are not performing well. SBI indicate to the investor, shareholder & creditors because both are profitable one as compare to other.

The Lehman brother went in liquidity in US and ICICI bank has also shared about Lehman brother so it also effect on ICICI bank. ICICI bank profit decrease on that reason and it lose credit from the customer.

SBI:-

From the comparative study on the basis of financial result, graph representation & also from the ratio interpretation I allow 1st Rank to State bank of India because ratio analysis such as, Dividend pay out ratio and current ratio and price of share and EPS is high as compare to other three banks & also earning per share is 103.94 and book value 776.48, price of share is 1413.

HDFC BANK:-

From the comparative study on the basis of financial result, graph representation & also from the ratio interpretation I allow 2 ranks to HDFC bank because ratio analysis such as EPS, ROA, ROE and Price Earning Ratio is good & also Book value is 324.39 and price of share is 1024.

ICICI BANK:-

From the comparative study on the basis of financial result, graph representation & also from the ratio interpretation I allows 3 rank to ICICI bank because ratio analysis such as Gross profit Ratio, Dividend Pay out Ratio, Price Earning Ratio is good and also Book value is 417.64 and price of share is 391.

BANK OF BARODA:-

From the comparative study on the basis of financial result, graph representation & also from the ratio interpretation I allow 4 rank to BOB because price of share, Price Earning ratio, EPS ,DPS less on compare to other three bank. Book value is 302.13 & Price is 304.

7. SUGGESTION FOR INVESTORS

1. The Investor should know how to analyze the share price of the company & pick up the under valued share.
2. Before investing he should undertake a deep study on the net sales, net profit in relation to equity capital employed and should attempt to forecast for coming years.
3. He should not invest his money in one or two company because if the companies' price decline, he will have to bear huge loss.
4. Ratio analysis, financial analysis, book value, earning per share, dividend pay out is useful tool for long term investment.
5. Follow market trend because it is the best way to get high return & minimize risk.

8. Limitation of the Study

1. Financial statement does note represent the complete picture of of the business but merely a collection of facts, which can be expressed in monetary term. They may not refer other factors, which affect the performance.
2. The report is prepared only on the basis of financial situation of the company and the other data. We can not have the 0ther important sources such as social position of the company in the market, its 4Ps, Labor policy which required for the whole research to get a better conclusion.
3. Insufficient time because of this limit period we have chosen 4 company for the sector so that could not find out form the overall point of view best investment opportunity in banking sector as there are many companies which are best for investment purpose.
4. Indian stock market is not stable it keep on fluctuation so ratio derived today may not consider as useful tool of valuation tomorrow.

9. CONCLUSION

Today scenario investor must be very careful to invest their money in each sector of Scrip's. I have selected 4 companies i.e. State bank of India, ICICI bank, HDFC bank and Bank of Baroda under the banking sector. The following rank is given on basis average of the current year and previous year.

Criteria/Rank	1	2	3	4
Current Ratio	SBI	BOB	ICICI	HDFC
Gross profit Margin	ICICI	BOB	SBI	HDFC
Net profit Margin	HDFC	SBI	ICICI	BOB
Return on Equity	HDFC	SBI	ICICI	BOB
Return on Assets	HDFC	ICICI	SBI	BOB
Earnings per Share	SBI	HDFC	ICICI	BOB
Dividends per Share	SBI	ICICI	HDFC	BOB
P/E ratio	HDFC	ICICI	SBI	BOB

D/P Ratio, EPS ,Current Ratio and Price of Share of SBI is higher than other bank , so it is best & Safe bank for investor to invest their money in banking sector.

10. Tables

HDFC BANK P & L A/C

Rs. in Crs.

Year	Mar 08	Mar 07	Mar 06
Interest Earned	10,115.00	6,647.93	4,475.34
Other Income	2,283.15	1,594.59	1,213.64
TOTAL	12,398.15	8,242.52	5,688.98
Interest expended	4,887.12	3,179.45	1,929.50
Operating Expenses	3,745.62	2,496.25	1,780.75
Provisions & Contingencies	2,175.23	1,425.37	1,107.95
TOTAL	10,807.97	7,101.07	4,818.20
Net Profit for the year	1,590.18	1,141.45	870.78
Prior Year Adjustments	0.00	0.00	0.00
Profit brought forward	1,932.03	1,455.02	602.34
TOTAL	3,522.21	2,596.47	1,473.12
Transfer to Statutory Reserves	397.55	285.36	217.70
Transfer to	197.58	117.51	-395.99

Other Reserves			
Proposed Dividend / Transfer to Government	352.47	261.57	196.39
Balance c/f to Balance Sheet	2,574.61	1,932.03	1,455.02
TOTAL	3,522.21	2,596.47	1,473.12
Equity Dividend	301.27	223.57	172.23
Corporate Dividend Tax	51.20	38.00	24.16
Equity Dividend (%)	85.00	70.00	55.00
Earning Per Share (Rs.)	43.42	34.55	27.04
Book Value	324.39	201.42	169.24
Extraordinary Items	0.43	-0.68	0.19

ICICI Bank P & L A/C

Rs. in Crs.

Year	Mar 08	Mar 07	Mar 06
Interest Earned	30,788.34	21,995.59	14,306.13
Other Income	8,878.85	6,962.95	5,062.22
TOTAL	39,667.19	28,958.54	19,368.35
Interest expended	23,484.24	16,358.50	9,597.45
Operating Expenses	8,222.27	6,725.63	5,856.89
Provisions & Contingencies	3,802.95	2,764.19	1,373.94
TOTAL	35,509.46	25,848.32	16,828.28
Net Profit for the year	4,157.73	3,110.22	2,540.07
Prior Year Adjustments	0.00	0.00	0.00
Profit brought forward	998.27	293.44	188.22
TOTAL	5,156.00	3,403.66	2,728.29
Transfer to Statutory Reserves	1,040.00	780.00	636.00
Transfer to Other Reserves	302.31	571.12	933.02
Proposed	1,377.37	1,054.27	865.83

Dividend / Transfer to Government			
Balance c/f to Balance Sheet	2,436.32	998.27	293.44
TOTAL	5,156.00	3,403.66	2,728.29
Equity Dividend	1,227.70	901.17	759.33
Corporate Dividend Tax	149.67	153.10	106.50
Equity Dividend (%)	110.00	100.00	85.00
Earning Per Share (Rs.)	36.02	32.88	27.35
Book Value	417.64	270.35	249.55
Extraordinary Items	45.23	85.37	5.60

State Bank of India P&L A/C

Rs. in Crs.

Year	Mar 08	Mar 07	Mar 06
Interest Earned	48,950.31	37,242.33	35,979.57
Other Income	9,487.11	7,429.04	7,528.16
TOTAL	58,437.42	44,671.37	43,507.73
Interest expended	31,929.08	22,184.13	20,390.45
Operating	13,312.11	12,464.24	11,759.65

Expenses			
Provisions & Contingencies	6,467.11	5,481.69	6,950.96
TOTAL	51,708.30	40,130.06	39,101.06
Net Profit for the year	6,729.12	4,541.31	4,406.67
Prior Year Adjustments	0.00	0.00	0.00
Profit brought forward	0.34	0.34	0.34
TOTAL	6,729.46	4,541.65	4,407.01
Transfer to Statutory Reserves	4,839.07	3,358.11	2,933.77
Transfer to Other Reserves	366.52	321.16	632.74
Proposed Dividend / Transfer to Government	1,523.53	862.04	840.16
Balance c/f to Balance Sheet	0.34	0.34	0.34
TOTAL	6,729.46	4,541.65	4,407.01
Equity Dividend	1,357.66	736.82	736.82
Corporate Dividend Tax	165.87	125.22	103.34
Equity	215.00	140.00	140.00

Dividend (%)			
Earning Per Share (Rs.)	103.94	83.91	81.77
Book Value	776.48	594.69	525.25
Extraordinary Items	7.00	4.52	1.37

Bank of Baroda P & L A/C

Rs.in Crs

Year	Mar 08	Mar 07	Mar 06
Interest Earned	11,813.48	9,004.09	7,049.95
Other Income	2,078.70	1,434.03	1,394.05
TOTAL	13,892.18	10,438.12	8,444.00
Interest expended	7,901.67	5,426.56	3,875.09
Operating Expenses	2,955.09	2,588.49	2,547.14
Provisions & Contingencies	1,599.90	1,396.61	1,194.81
TOTAL	12,456.66	9,411.66	7,617.04
Net Profit for the year	1,435.52	1,026.46	826.96
Prior Year Adjustments	0.00	0.00	0.00
Profit brought forward	0.00	0.00	0.00
TOTAL	1,435.52	1,026.46	826.96

Transfer to Statutory Reserves	359.58	257.19	206.74
Transfer to Other Reserves	735.00	516.81	412.54
Proposed Dividend / Transfer to Government	340.94	252.46	207.68
Balance c/f to Balance Sheet	0.00	0.00	0.00
TOTAL	1,435.52	1,026.46	826.96
Equity Dividend	291.42	218.56	182.14
Corporate Dividend Tax	49.52	33.90	25.54
Equity Dividend (%)	80.00	60.00	50.00
Earning Per Share (Rs.)	37.92	27.15	21.92
Book Value	302.13	236.64	214.60
Extraordinary Items	0.22	8.01	-0.20

Bank of Baroda Balance sheet

Rs. in crs.

Year	Mar 08	Mar 07	Mar 06
Capital	365.53	365.53	365.53
Reserves and Surplus	10,678.40	8,284.41	7,478.91
Deposits	152,034.13	124,915.98	93,661.99
Borrowings	3,927.05	1,142.56	4,802.20
Other Liabilities & Provisions	12,594.41	8,437.70	7,083.90
TOTAL	179,599.52	143,146.18	113,392.53
Cash & Balances with RBI	9,369.72	6,413.52	3,333.43
Balances with Banks & money at Call & Short Notice	12,929.57	11,866.85	10,121.21
Investments	43,870.07	34,943.63	35,114.22
Advances	106,701.32	83,620.87	59,911.78
Fixed	2,427.01	1,088.81	920.73

Assets			
Other Assets	4,301.83	5,212.50	3,991.16
TOTAL	179,599.52	143,146.18	113,392.53
Contingent Liabilities	82,362.32	61,375.32	39,200.54
Bills for collection	8,315.02	6,627.59	5,895.61

State Bank of India Balance sheet

Rs. in crs

Year	Mar 08	Mar 07	Mar 06
Capital	631.47	526.30	526.30
Reserves and Surplus	48,401.19	30,772.26	27,117.79
Deposits	537,403.94	435,521.09	380,046.06
Borrowings	51,727.41	39,703.33	30,641.24
Other Liabilities & Provisions	83,961.07	60,283.15	55,829.23
TOTAL	722,125.08	566,806.13	494,160.62
Cash & Balances with RBI	51,534.61	29,076.43	21,652.70
Balances with Banks	15,931.72	22,892.26	22,907.30

& money at Call & Short Notice			
Investments	189,501.27	149,148.88	162,534.24
Advances	416,768.20	337,336.49	261,800.94
Fixed Assets	3,373.48	2,818.87	2,752.93
Other Assets	45,015.80	25,533.20	22,512.51
TOTAL	722,125.08	566,806.13	494,160.62
Contingent Liabilities	810,796.48	526,954.66	228,881.38
Bills for collection	18,946.80	23,367.51	20,592.95

HDFC Bank Balance sheet

Rs. in crs

Year	Mar 08	Mar 07	Mar 06
Capital	354.43	319.39	313.14
Reserves and Surplus	11,142.80	6,113.76	4,986.39
Deposits	100,768.60	68,297.94	55,796.82
Borrowings	4,478.86	2,815.39	2,858.48
Other Liabilities &	16,506.32	13,772.81	9,632.04

Provisions			
TOTAL	133,251.01	91,319.29	73,586.87
Cash & Balances with RBI	12,553.18	5,075.25	3,306.61
Balances with Banks & money at Call & Short Notice	2,225.16	3,971.40	3,612.39
Investments	49,393.54	30,564.80	28,393.96
Advances	63,426.90	46,944.78	35,061.26
Fixed Assets	1,175.13	966.67	855.08
Other Assets	4,477.10	3,796.39	2,357.57
TOTAL	133,251.01	91,319.29	73,586.87
Contingent Liabilities	593,008.08	328,148.24	214,782.34
Bills for collection	6,920.71	4,606.83	2,828.89

ICICI Bank Balance sheet

Rs. in crs

Year	Mar 08	Mar 07	Mar 06
Capital	1,462.68	1,249.34	1,239.83
Reserves and Surplus	45,357.53	23,413.92	21,316.16
Deposits	244,431.05	230,510.19	165,083.17
Borrowings	65,648.43	51,256.03	38,521.91
Other Liabilities & Provisions	43,517.43	38,882.96	25,897.60
TOTAL	400,417.12	345,312.44	252,058.67
Cash & Balances with RBI	29,377.53	18,706.88	8,934.37
Balances with Banks & money at Call & Short Notice	8,663.60	18,414.44	8,105.85
Investment	111,454.34	91,257.84	71,547.39

s			
Advances	225,616.08	195,865.60	146,163.11
Fixed Assets	4,108.90	3,923.42	3,980.71
Other Assets	21,196.67	17,144.26	13,327.24
TOTAL	400,417.12	345,312.44	252,058.67
Contingent Liabilities	1,151,349.01	562,959.91	395,033.67
Bills for collection	4,278.28	4,046.56	4,338.46

11. Bibliography

- **Website:**
    1. www.icici.com
    2. www.sbi.com
    3. www.hdfc.com
    4. www.bob.com
    5. www.moneypore.com
    6. www.moneycontrol.com
    7. www.bse.com
    8. www.indiafinance.com

- **Book & Magzine**

    1. Fundamental Analysis-Taxman
    2. Business World
    3. Financial Management-Khan & Jain

www.ingramcontent.com/pod-product-compliance
Lightning Source LLC
Chambersburg PA
CBHW071119210326
41519CB00020B/6344